NATIONAL GEOGRAPHIC KiDS

weird but true! 8

THAT'S WEIRD!

THE CROWNED SIFAKA— A **LEMUR** THAT LIVES IN MADAGASCAR— EATS **DIRT**.

An **earthquake** made **Mount Everest** about an **inch shorter.**

(2.5 cm)

There are as many molecules in **ten drops** of **water** as there are **stars** in the universe.

KANGAROOS USE THEIR TAILS AS AN EXTRA LEG WHEN WALKING.

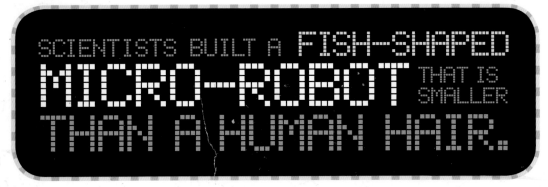

SCIENTISTS BUILT A FISH-SHAPED MICRO-ROBOT THAT IS SMALLER THAN A HUMAN HAIR.

A **FARMER** FROM MASSACHUSETTS, U.S.A., ONCE PADDLED DOWN A RIVER IN AN **817-POUND** (371-kg) HOLLOWED-OUT **PUMPKIN.**

A compound in **human spit** can help **heal wounds.**

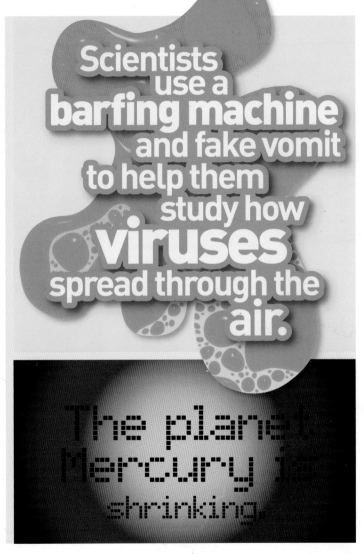

Scientists use a **barfing machine** and fake vomit to help them study how **viruses** spread through the air.

The planet Mercury is shrinking.

9

LUKE SKYWALKER'S **LIGHTSABER** HAS ACTUALLY BEEN TO **SPACE.**

ONE MAN OWNS **500,000** PIECES OF *STAR WARS*

The sound of
**Darth Vader's
breathing**
was inspired by breathing
apparatuses used for
scuba diving.

MEMORABILIA—THE LARGEST COLLECTION IN THE WORLD.

A WATERFALL IN MINNESOTA, U.S.A., DROPS INTO A DEEP HOLE AND DISAPPEARS. NO ONE KNOWS WHERE THE WATER GOES.

A GIANT BLACK HOLE ATE A STAR AND BURPED OUT A FLAME.

SOME OF THE EARLIEST BOATS WERE MADE FROM PLANTS.

Dragonflies can fly straight up and down and hover in midair like a helicopter.

A NOW EXTINCT FROG SPECIES SWALLOWED ITS EGGS, INCUBATED THEM IN ITS STOMACH, AND GAVE BIRTH THROUGH ITS MOUTH.

14

ALL MAMMALS HEAVIER THAN 6.6 POUNDS (3 kg) **TAKE THE SAME AMOUNT OF TIME TO PEE.**

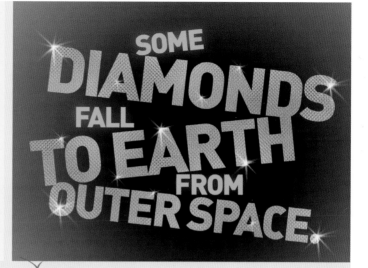

SOME **DIAMONDS** FALL **TO EARTH** FROM **OUTER SPACE.**

Plants talk to one another through an underground network of fungi.

YOU NEED A **FOOT-LONG STICK,** (0.3-m) A **THREE-POUND PUCK,** (1.4-kg) AND **SNORKEL GEAR** TO **PLAY UNDERWATER HOCKEY.**

ONLY ABOUT 10 PERCENT OF THE POPULATION IS LEFT-HANDED.

Drinking *coffee* in 17th-century *Turkey* was punishable by *death.*

YOUR BODY'S SMELL—OR "ODORPRINT"—IS AS UNIQUE AS YOUR FINGERPRINTS.

WEEEE!

As part of a **beaver-relocation effort,** **76 beavers** once **parachuted** into the Idaho, U.S.A., wilderness.

Raindrops are shaped like pancakes.

SCIENTISTS SAY YOUR GUT HAS A "BRAIN."

Ants give themselves medicine when they get sick.

20

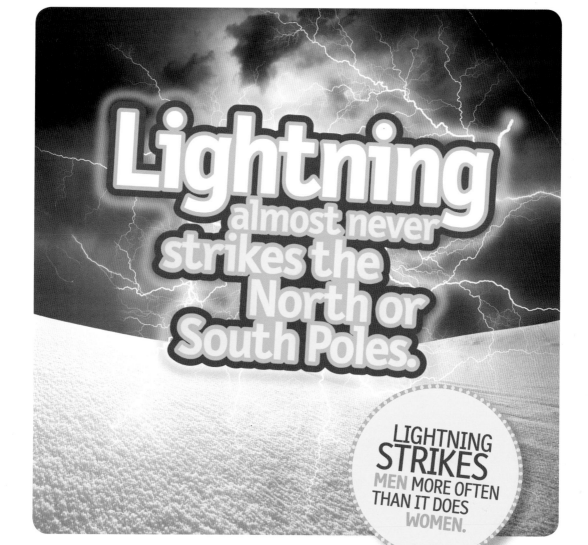

Lightning
almost never strikes the North or South Poles.

LIGHTNING **STRIKES** MEN MORE OFTEN THAN IT DOES WOMEN.

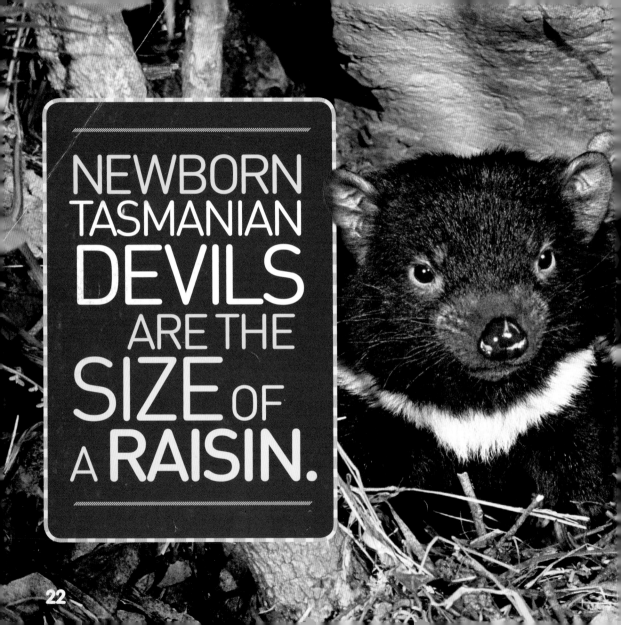

NEWBORN TASMANIAN DEVILS ARE THE SIZE OF A RAISIN.

Jellyfish invasions have shut down nuclear power plants.

There's an app that lets people **rent** out their **toilets.**

SCIENTISTS FOUND **PREHISTORIC VIRUSES** IN **SIBERIAN ICE.**

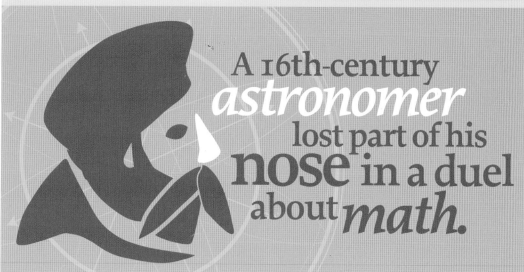

A 16th-century *astronomer* lost part of his **nose** in a duel about *math.*

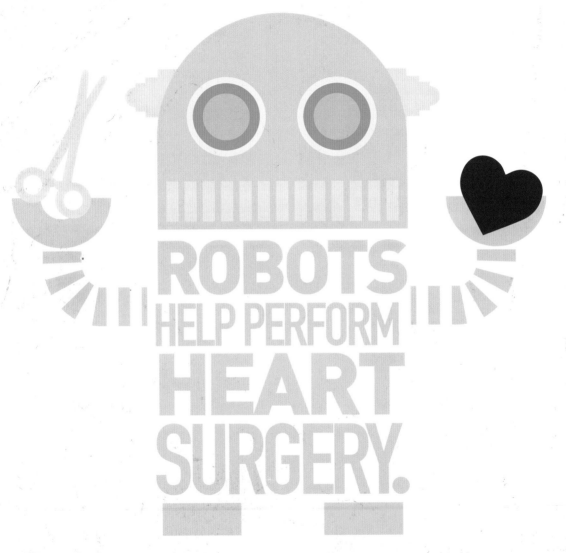

ROBOTS HELP PERFORM HEART SURGERY.

THE HUBBLE SPACE TELESCOPE CAN LOOK BACK IN TIME.

Mushrooms are also called toadstools.

NEANDERTHALS FLOSSED THEIR TEETH WITH TWIGS AND BLADES OF GRASS.

peecycling = using urine to fertilize vegetables

RESEARCHERS HAVE DEVELOPED 3-D GLASSES FOR INSECTS.

A STUDY FOUND THAT **CHILDREN** WHOSE FAMILIES **WASH DISHES BY HAND** HAVE **FEWER ALLERGIES** THAN KIDS WHOSE FAMILIES **USE A DISHWASHER.**

31

Wolf pups can't see or hear when they're born.

You are made of star dust.

Some plants can hear themselves being eaten.

There was only one student in New Mexico State University's first graduating class.

a nighttime rainbow

41

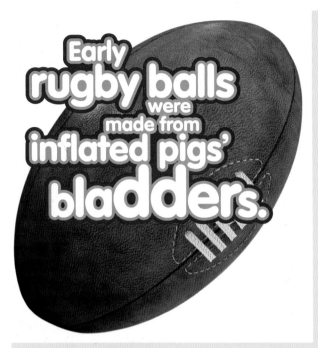

Early **rugby balls** were made from **inflated pigs' bladders.**

2015 was the International Year of Light.

SCIENTISTS HAVE DISCOVERED A **PROTEIN** THAT CAN PREVENT **ICE CREAM** FROM **MELTING** QUICKLY IN HOT WEATHER.

THE BOARD GAME MONOPOLY

WAS ORIGINALLY CALLED
THE LANDLORD'S GAME.

MONOPOLY
IS BASED ON
STREET NAMES
IN ATLANTIC CITY,
NEW JERSEY, U.S.A.

FAMOUS

HORROR-FILM DIRECTOR

ALFRED

HITCHCOCK

WAS AFRAID OF

EGGS.

U.S. president James A. Garfield was fond of **squirrel soup.**

FEMALE **PHARAOHS** WORE FAKE BEARDS.

Scientists made medicine out of cockroach brain cells.

SAY WHAT?!

Elephants have fingers on the end of their trunks.

POPE LEO X **BURIED** HIS

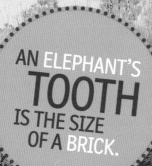

AN ELEPHANT'S **TOOTH** IS THE SIZE OF A BRICK.

PET ELEPHANT **UNDER** THE VATICAN.

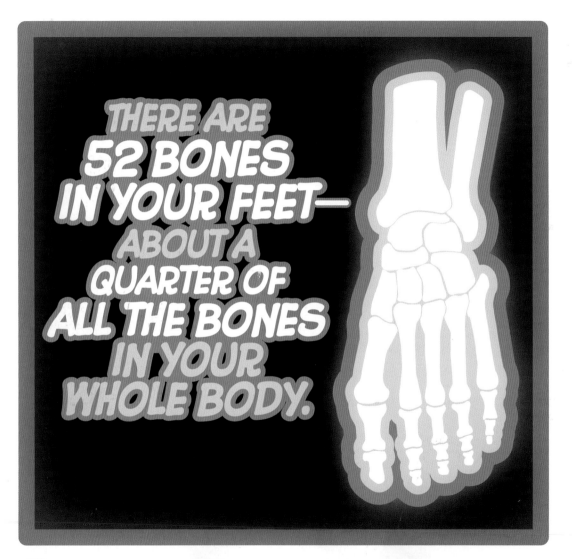

THERE ARE 52 BONES IN YOUR FEET— ABOUT A QUARTER OF ALL THE BONES IN YOUR WHOLE BODY.

VANILLA IS USED TO MAKE CHOCOLATE.

Some **dogs' paws** smell like **corn chips.**

AFTER THEIR 1972 NATIONAL HOCKEY LEAGUE WIN, THE BOSTON BRUINS'S NAME WAS MISSPELLED "BQSTQN BRUINS" ON THE STANLEY CUP.

THERE'S A ROCK ON MARS THAT LOOKS LIKE A FLOATING SPOON.

AN EAR OF CORN CAN HAVE UP TO 1,200 KERNELS.

A **LIBROCUBICULARIST** IS SOMEONE WHO **READS IN BED.**

Police "arrested" a goat for loitering outside a doughnut shop in Saskatchewan, Canada.

53

There are more than **40,000** types of rice.

If you strung together all the **cranberries** grown in North America **in one year,** they would stretch from Boston to Los Angeles, U.S.A., more than **500 times.**

SHEEP SHEARING IS A COMPETITIVE SPORT.

THERE IS A
BODY OF
WATER
FLOATING IN
OUTER SPACE
THAT'S
140 TRILLION
TIMES
BIGGER
THAN ALL THE
EARTH'S
OCEANS
COMBINED.

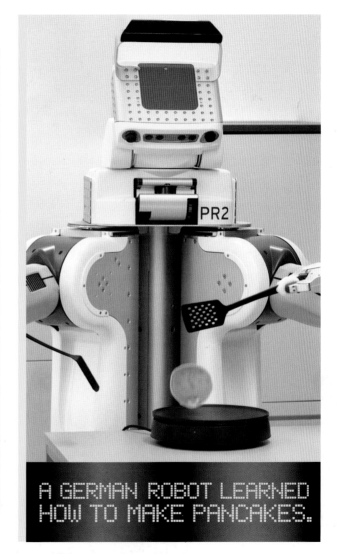

A GERMAN ROBOT LEARNED HOW TO MAKE PANCAKES.

penny farthing= a bicycle with a giant **front wheel** and a tiny back wheel

Fastest one-mile run (1.6-km) by a human wearing swim fins: 5 minutes and 48.86 seconds

During Olympic training, **swimmer** Michael Phelps consumed more than **12,000 calories** a day—about the equivalent of **80 cups of whole milk.** (18.9 L)

CHRISTOPHER COLUMBUS BROUGHT THE FIRST **LEMON SEEDS** TO THE AMERICAS.

PARTS OF CALIFORNIA, U.S.A., ARE SINKING.

IN NEW ZEALAND, PARENTS AREN'T ALLOWED TO NAME THEIR BABIES AFTER PUNCTUATION MARKS.

" ! ? ; - , (:) [,] ' { . . . }.

A HONEYBEE HAS THE SAME NUMBER OF HAIRS AS A SQUIRREL: THREE MILLION.

SCIENTISTS ARE DEVELOPING ROBOT BEES

HONEY
HAS BEEN FOUND
IN THE
CENTER OF OLD
GOLF BALLS.

THAT COULD ARTIFICIALLY POLLINATE CROPS.

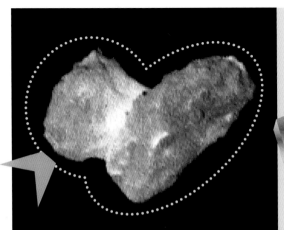

There's a **comet** shaped like a **rubber duck.**

CHOCOLATE WAS ONCE USED AS MONEY.

Some **snakes pass gas** in **self-defense.**

Painting was once an Olympic event.

One in four medicines comes from rain forest plants.

The world's first speeding **ticket** was given to a motorist going *eight* miles an hour.
(12.9 km/h)

The 1904 World's Fair featured a life-size elephant made of almonds.

BACTERIA TALK TO EACH OTHER.

"chicken wing" = a bad golf swing

The city of Redondo Beach, California, U.S.A., once chose a **blimp** as its **official bird.**

SNAILS SMELL WITH THEIR LIPS.

TO ENSURE THEY HAVEN'T BEEN SWITCHED OR TAMPERED WITH, ALL EGGS USED IN THE COMPETITIVE SPORT OF EGG THROWING ARE MARKED FOR SECURITY PURPOSES.

"FRIED EGG"=THE WAY A GOLF

SCIENTISTS HAVE FIGURED OUT HOW TO UNBOIL AN EGG.

BALL SOMETIMES LANDS IN A SAND TRAP

Einstein never wore socks.

Humans and dogs perform together in a sport called musical canine freestyle.

Earmuffs *were invented by a* **teenage** *boy in* 1858.

Some orchids smell like human body odor to attract mosquitoes.

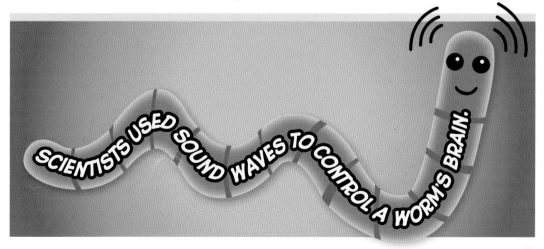

SCIENTISTS USED SOUND WAVES TO CONTROL A WORM'S BRAIN.

DEATH METAL MUSIC ATTRACTS SHARKS.

IN NEW ZEALAND, YOU CAN **PLAY GOLF** WITH **FOOTBALL-SHAPED GOLF BALLS.**

Some scientists think that **plants** can learn.

Spiders can build **webs** that are a half mile long.
(0.8 km)

An artist created an **18-foot-long** (5.5-m) **Batmobile** out of more than **500,000** Lego bricks.

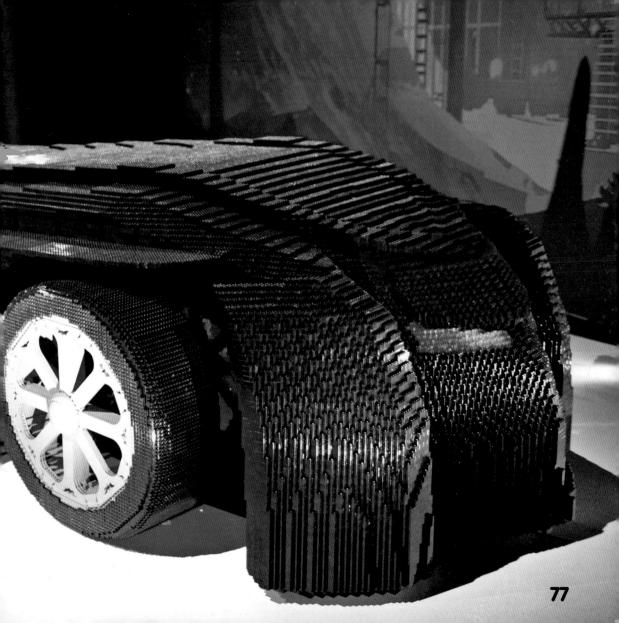

Tooth enamel evolved from **ancient fish scales.**

An **aglet** is the **plastic piece** at the end of **your shoelace.**

Fidgeting can make you healthier.

snood = the flesh that hangs down over a male **turkey's beak**

TOMATOES CAN BE PURPLE.

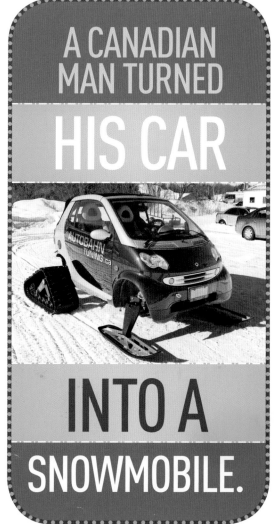

A CANADIAN MAN TURNED **HIS CAR** INTO A SNOWMOBILE.

Some **carnivorous plants** can **eat** birds.

During his 1905 U.S. presidential inauguration, *Teddy Roosevelt* wore *a ring* containing a lock of **Abraham Lincoln's** *hair.*

Your brain produces enough **electricity** to power a 40-watt **lightbulb** for an entire **day.**

HUMMINGBIRDS USE **HAWKS** FOR PROTECTION.

moonbow=

There are approximately **3 trillion** (3,000,000,000,000) trees on Earth.

ONE RARE PLANT GROWS ONLY ON TOP OF DIAMOND DEPOSITS.

THAT'S WEIRD!

A **BROWN BAT** CAN EAT
1,000 MOSQUITOES
IN AN HOUR.

People in one small **Turkish** *town* communicate *over long distances by* **whistling.**

A MAN SUED THE KELLOGG COMPANY BECAUSE HE FOUND NO REAL FRUIT IN HIS FROOT LOOPS CEREAL.

SCIENTISTS THINK **T. REX** WAS A CANNIBAL.

GLOBAL WARMING IS CHANGING THE SHAPE OF THE PLANET.

THE LONGEST PIZZA

EVER MADE WAS ALMOST A **MILE LONG.**
(1.6 km)

IT WAS MADE WITH **1.5 TONS** (1.4 t) OF **MOZZARELLA** AND **2 TONS** (1.8 t) OF **TOMATO SAUCE.**

Kids grow faster in the springtime.

A **caterpillar's body** has **more muscles** than a human's.

baboon = a type of lemon

HAVING A FULL BLADDER MAKES YOU A BETTER LIAR.

Bonobos **blow** raspberries for attention.

LISTENING TO ROCK MUSIC WHILE EATING CAN MAKE FOOD TASTE SPICIER, ONE STUDY FOUND.

In China you can order dried-pork-and-seaweed-flavored doughnuts.

SOME BABY SPIDERS EAT THEIR MOTHER.

Computers can be programmed to recognize emotions in stories.

A FROG NAMED SANTJIE MADE THE LONGEST RECORDED JUMP— 33 FEET 5.5 INCHES (10.2 m) AT A FROG DERBY IN SOUTH AFRICA.

T string parts band are c phloen (FLO-em

ONE OF MARS'S MOONS IS FALLING APART.

Prairie dogs say hello with kisses.

VIRGA IS RAIN THAT EVAPORATES BEFORE IT HITS THE GROUND.

PLANTS CAN GET FEVERS.

A man named **Santa Claus** once ran for city council in North Pole, Alaska, U.S.A.

The average **tornado** is on the ground for only **five minutes.**

King Henry III of England had a **pet bear** that swam in the Thames River and caught fish.

CAMEL MILK DOESN'T CURDLE.

"Albert Einstein" and "Ten Elite Brains" have all the **same letters,** just rearranged.

A **200-year-old** Chinese giant salamander weighing more than **100 pounds** (45 kg) was found in **a cave—alive.**

93

An **artist** covered an entire **city bus** with **yarn.**

扇沢ー黒部ダム

Jousting is the *official sport*

of the U.S. state of Maryland.

PUMPKINS
ALMOST WENT
EXTINCT.

THE STATE VEGETABLE OF OKLAHOMA, U.S.A., IS THE WATERMELON.

Bonobos blow raspberries for attention.

LISTENING TO ROCK MUSIC WHILE EATING CAN MAKE FOOD TASTE SPICIER, ONE STUDY FOUND.

In China you can order dried-pork-and-seaweed-**flavored doughnuts.**

SOME **BABY SPIDERS** EAT THEIR **MOTHER.**

Computers can be programmed to recognize emotions in stories.

A FROG NAMED SANTJIE MADE THE LONGEST RECORDED JUMP— 33 FEET 5.5 INCHES (10.2 m) AT A FROG DERBY IN SOUTH AFRICA.

The stringy parts of a banana are called phloem (FLO-em).

A **caterpillar's body** has **more muscles** than a human's.

baboon= a type of lemon

HAVING A FULL BLADDER MAKES YOU A BETTER LIAR.

An **artist** covered an entire **city bus** with **yarn.**

CAMEL MILK DOESN'T CURDLE.

"Albert Einstein" and "Ten Elite Brains" have all the **same letters,** just rearranged.

A **200-year-old** Chinese giant salamander weighing more than **100 pounds** was found in (45 kg) a cave—alive.

The U.S. state of **Kansas** produces enough **wheat** every year to make **35 billion** loaves of bread.

HUMANS HAVE EXPLORED LESS

THAN 5 PERCENT OF THE OCEAN.

earworm = a song that gets stuck in your head

The first living things on Earth were **bacteria.**

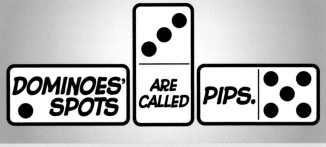

DOMINOES' SPOTS ARE CALLED PIPS.

A man in Spain has ribs made by a 3-D printer.

THE SUN HAS HOLES IN IT.

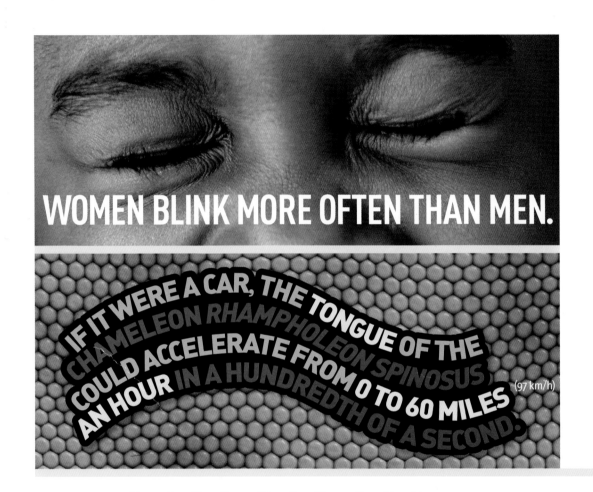

WOMEN BLINK MORE OFTEN THAN MEN.

IF IT WERE A CAR, THE TONGUE OF THE CHAMELEON RHAMPHOLEON SPINOSUS COULD ACCELERATE FROM 0 TO 60 MILES AN HOUR IN A HUNDREDTH OF A SECOND. (97 km/h)

ABOUT 9,000,000,000 PIECES OF

THE SUN HAS HOLES IN IT.

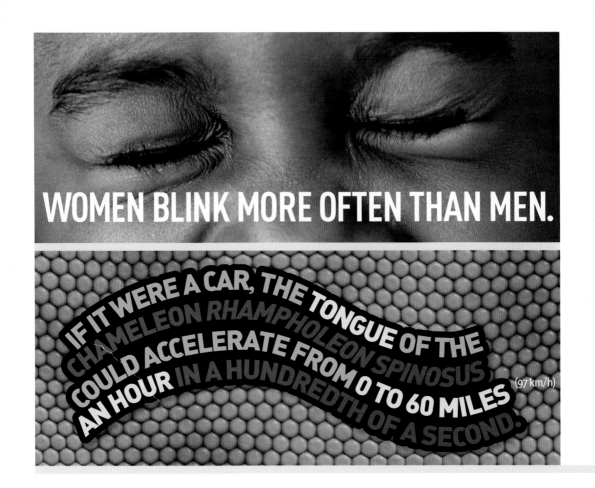

WOMEN BLINK MORE OFTEN THAN MEN.

IF IT WERE A CAR, THE TONGUE OF THE CHAMELEON RHAMPHOLEON SPINOSUS COULD ACCELERATE FROM 0 TO 60 MILES AN HOUR IN A HUNDREDTH OF A SECOND. (97 km/h)

ABOUT 9,000,000,000 PIECES OF

CANDY CORN WILL BE MADE THIS YEAR.

U.S. PRESIDENT WOODROW WILSON KEPT A FLOCK OF SHEEP ON THE WHITE HOUSE LAWN.

baaa

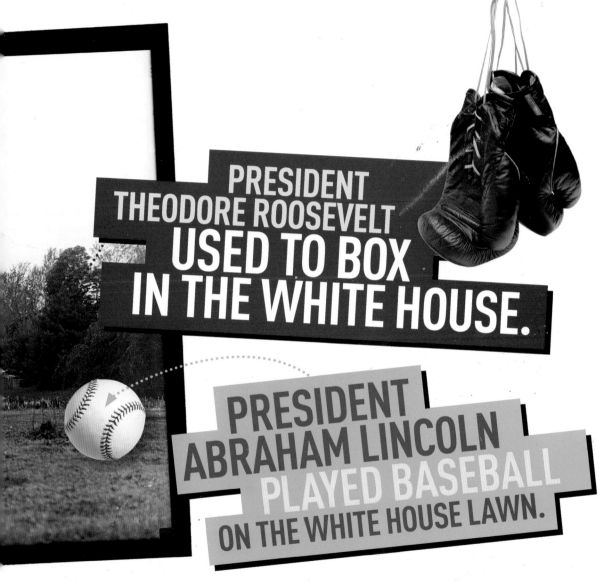

PRESIDENT THEODORE ROOSEVELT **USED TO BOX IN THE WHITE HOUSE.**

PRESIDENT ABRAHAM LINCOLN PLAYED BASEBALL ON THE WHITE HOUSE LAWN.

SNAKES ONCE HAD LEGS.

A U.S. UNIVERSITY HAS THOUSANDS OF **BRAINS** STORED IN A **BRAIN BANK.**

The most expensive car ever sold went for $34.65 million.

The sea bunny is actually a slug.

PLUTO
IS ONLY ABOUT HALF AS WIDE AS THE UNITED STATES.

YOUR TASTE BUDS GO NUMB WHEN YOU FLY.

AMERICA'S FIRST ROLLER COASTER HAULED COAL IN THE MORNING AND PEOPLE IN THE AFTERNOON.

RESEARCHERS FOUND A NEW SPECIES OF **SPIDER THAT PLAYS PEEKABOO TO ATTRACT MATES.**

ONLY ONE PERCENT OF ALL THE

WATER
ON EARTH
IS FIT FOR HUMAN USE.

No one really knows why **humans** have to **sleep.**

Scientists designed a **tractor beam** that can pick up and move small objects using sound waves.

THE EARTH IS MOVING AWAY FROM THE SUN.

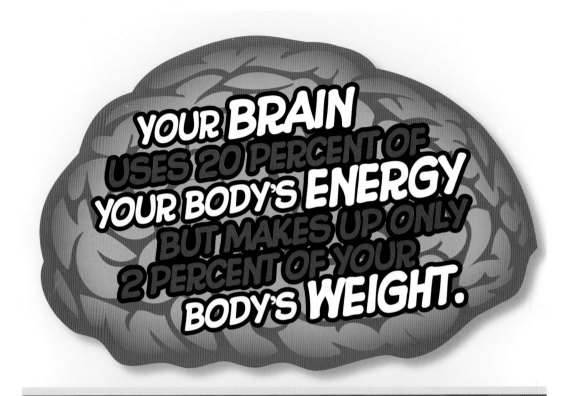

YOUR **BRAIN** USES 20 PERCENT OF YOUR BODY'S **ENERGY** BUT MAKES UP ONLY 2 PERCENT OF YOUR BODY'S **WEIGHT.**

A CHINESE ASTRONOMER INVENTED AN **EARTHQUAKE DETECTOR** IN A.D. 132.

ONE SPECIES
OF BIRD

TAP DANCES

I'VE GOT DANCIN' FEET!

TO ATTRACT

A MATE.

A **ten-gallon cowboy hat** holds only three (2.8 L) quarts of water.

SOUR PATCH KIDS WERE ORIGINALLY CALLED MARS MEN.

117

AUTOMOBILES ARE THE

MOST RECYCLED PRODUCT
IN THE UNITED STATES.

POODLES ARE BANNED FROM COMPETING IN THE IDITAROD.

120

The world's heaviest **turnip** weighed as much as a four-year-old **kid.**

THE AVERAGE AMERICAN EATS ABOUT A TON OF FOOD EACH YEAR. (0.9 t)

SCIENTISTS MADE A BATTERY USING **MUSHROOMS.**

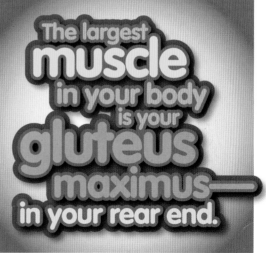

The largest **muscle** in your body is your **gluteus maximus**— in your rear end.

An Australian man once tried to auction off the country of New Zealand online.

Too much **oxygen** can make **you sick.**

GRAB A BITE IN ONE OF THESE U.S. TOWNS:

OATMEAL, TEXAS

SANDWICH, MASSACHUSETTS

PIE TOWN, NEW MEXICO

BURNT CORN, ALABAMA

CHICKEN, ALASKA

COOKIETOWN, OKLAHOMA

You become temporarily **paralyzed** while you dream.

123

214 PEOPLE FIT INSIDE THE WORLD'S LARGEST **SOAP BUBBLE.**

HORSES DON'T THROW UP.

THE **SNICKERS BAR** WAS NAMED AFTER A HORSE.

HORSES DON'T THROW UP.

THE **SNICKERS BAR** WAS NAMED AFTER A HORSE.

Starburst candies were invented in the United Kingdom and were originally called Opal Fruits.

spitters *sneesl* *snaw*

THERE ARE MORE THAN 400 WORDS FOR SNOW IN SCOTLAND.

flindrikin *skelf* *unbrak* *feefle*

OCTOBER 9 IS NATIONAL MOLDY ⋆⋆⋆ CHEESE DAY IN THE U.S.

An ancient *Chinese warrior* is said to have **stunned enemy troops** into retreat by *juggling nine balls* at once.

U.S. PRESIDENT BARACK OBAMA'S **DOG BO IS FEATURED ON A BASEBALL CARD.**

BURMA, LIBERIA, AND THE UNITED STATES **ARE THE ONLY COUNTRIES IN THE WORLD THAT HAVEN'T ADOPTED THE METRIC SYSTEM.**

Starburst candies were invented in the United Kingdom and were originally called Opal Fruits.

spitters *sneesl* *snaw*

THERE ARE MORE THAN 400 WORDS FOR SNOW IN SCOTLAND.

flindrikin *skelf* *unbrak* *feefle*

OCTOBER 9 IS NATIONAL MOLDY CHEESE DAY IN THE U.S.

An ancient *Chinese warrior* is said to have **stunned enemy troops** into retreat by *juggling nine balls* at once.

U.S. PRESIDENT BARACK OBAMA'S DOG BO IS FEATURED ON A BASEBALL CARD.

BURMA, LIBERIA, AND THE UNITED STATES **ARE THE ONLY COUNTRIES IN THE WORLD THAT HAVEN'T ADOPTED THE METRIC SYSTEM.**

6

5

4

3

2

1

Scientists found sharks living in an underwater volcano.

The entire land area of the United States could fit in the Sahara desert.

Some people in Ontario, Canada, ice-skate to work.

Chocolate comes from a fruit tree.

Arica, Chile, once went **14 years** with no **rainfall.**

New England **clam chowder** is the **official state dish** of **Massachusetts, U.S.A.**

44,000 CANS OF SPAM ARE MADE EVERY HOUR.

PILOTS AND COPILOTS EAT DIFFERENT FOOD OFF THE IN-FLIGHT MENU IN CASE ONE OF THE MEALS MAKES THEM SICK.

Americans renamed **sauerkraut** "Liberty Cabbage" during World War I.

A WOMAN IN CHINA GREW HER HAIR THREE TIMES LONGER THAN SHE WAS TALL.

AN ANCIENT FLYING REPTILE HAD A WINGSPAN ABOUT AS WIDE AS A FIGHTER JET.

The **oldest pieces of paper** in the world are **4,600** years old.

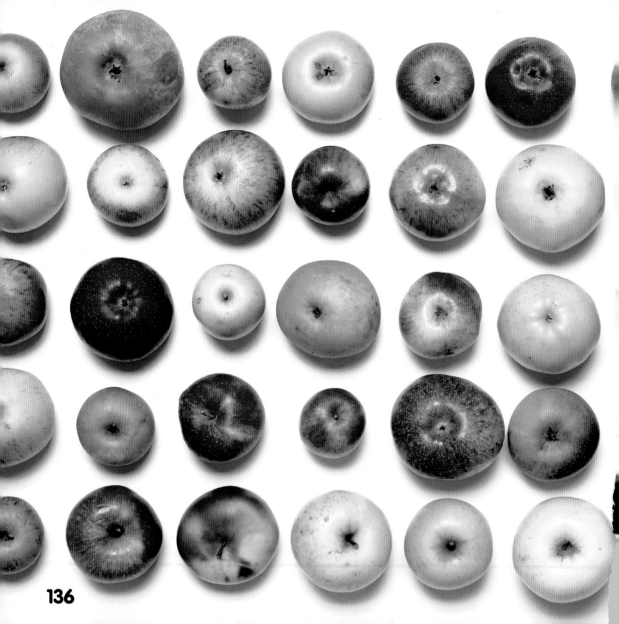

If you ate **one variety** of **apple per day,** it would take you more than **20 years** to try all the different kinds.

AMERICANS WILL EAT MORE THAN **6,000 PIECES OF PIZZA** IN A LIFETIME.

TOENAIL CLIPPINGS FROM MORE THAN **100,000 PEOPLE** ARE STASHED IN BASEMENT FREEZERS AT HARVARD UNIVERSITY.

The country of Tonga once had banana-shaped postage stamps.

AN ARTIST ONCE RE-CREATED THE "MONA LISA" USING ONLY PIECES OF TOAST.

"EMOTION RECOGNITION" SOFTWARE DETERMINED THAT THE "MONA LISA" IS 83 PERCENT HAPPY, 9 PERCENT DISGUSTED, 6 PERCENT FEARFUL, AND 2 PERCENT ANGRY.

The **50-star American flag** was designed by a high school student. His teacher gave him a B minus.

DISNEYLAND, IN CALIFORNIA, U.S.A., IS BIGGER THAN THE WORLD'S SMALLEST COUNTRY.

SOME OF THE BIGGEST PYRAMIDS

IN THE WORLD ARE IN MEXICO.

◀ A MAYA PYRAMID IN CHIAPAS, MEXICO

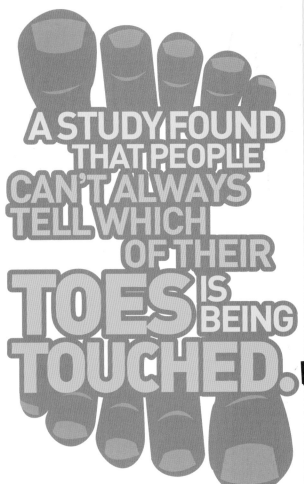

A STUDY FOUND THAT PEOPLE CAN'T ALWAYS TELL WHICH OF THEIR TOES IS BEING TOUCHED.

YOU FORGET MOST OF YOUR DREAMS.

A woman in England dug up a **potato** shaped like a duck.

quack

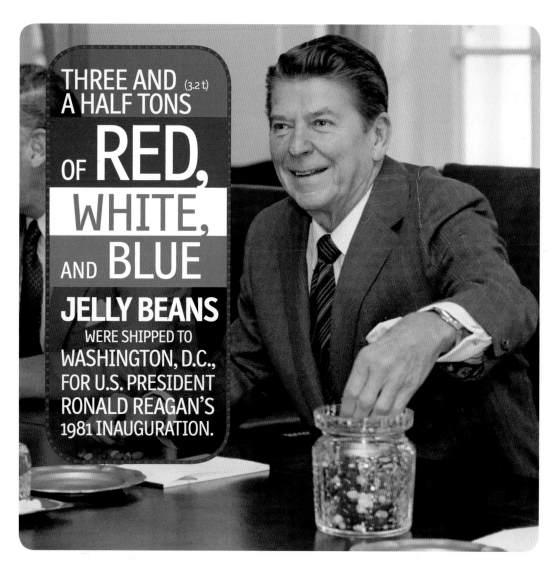

THREE AND (3.2 t) A HALF TONS OF **RED,** **WHITE,** AND **BLUE** **JELLY BEANS** WERE SHIPPED TO WASHINGTON, D.C., FOR U.S. PRESIDENT RONALD REAGAN'S 1981 INAUGURATION.

Dinosaurs may have danced to attract mates.

Some **turtles glow** in the dark.

PINK LEMONADE WAS INVENTED BY ACCIDENT, WHEN A LEMONADE SELLER DROPPED **RED CINNAMON CANDIES** INTO HIS LEMONADE, TURNING IT **PINK.**

Octopuses have blue blood.

OCTOPUSES HAVE **NINE** BRAINS.

Giraffes hum at night.

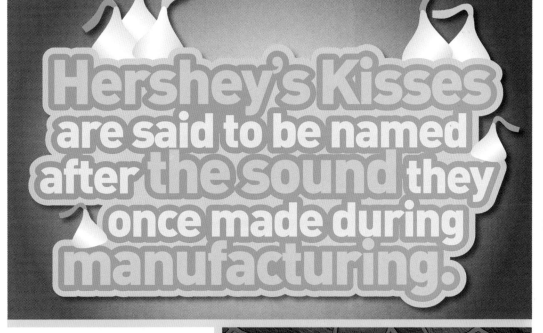

Hershey's Kisses are said to be named after the sound they once made during manufacturing.

SCIENTISTS FOUND **2.5-MILLION-YEAR-OLD** FOSSILIZED **PEACH PITS** IN CHINA.

THE **WALL** OF A MEDIEVAL CASTLE WAS FOUND UNDER **A PRISON** IN ENGLAND.

ONE AIRPLANE CAN CONTAIN 330 MILES OF WIRES.

(531 km)

A fast-food chain once sold a **hamburger** that turned people's poop **green.**

Microlattice— the world's lightest metal— is **99.99** percent **air.**

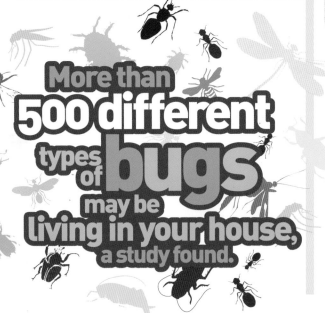

More than **500 different** types of **bugs** may be living in your house, a study found.

PHILTRUM

PHILTRUM

A fast-food chain once sold a **hamburger** that turned people's poop **green.**

More than **500 different** types of **bugs** may be living in your house, a study found.

Microlattice—the world's lightest metal—is **99.99** percent **air.**

THE GROOVE BETWEEN THE TOP OF YOUR UPPER LIP AND THE BOTTOM OF YOUR NOSE

AUSTRALIAN SCIENTISTS MADE SWIMSUITS FOR SEA TURTLES.

A truck carrying onions once caught fire near Frying Pan Road in Texas, U.S.A. (The driver got away safely.)

A WHALE **FOSSIL** WAS FOUND ON TOP OF A **MOUNTAIN.**

Some people are paid to **sniff** out the source of disgusting **smells.**

IT WOULD TAKE YOU ALMOST SIX MONTHS TO DRIVE A CAR FROM EARTH TO THE MOON AT 60 MILES AN HOUR. (97 km/h)

TURKEYS WERE CONSIDERED SACRED BY EARLY NATIVE AMERICANS.

THERE WAS A COCKROACH HALL OF FAME IN PLANO, TEXAS, U.S.A.

Blue is the most popular toothbrush color.

IT TOOK UP TO **SEVEN PEOPLE TO OPERATE THE GIANT JABBA THE HUTT PUPPET** FROM THE *STAR WARS* MOVIES.

During a **drought,** the city of Los Angeles dropped **96 million plastic "shade balls"** into a reservoir to keep the water from evaporating.

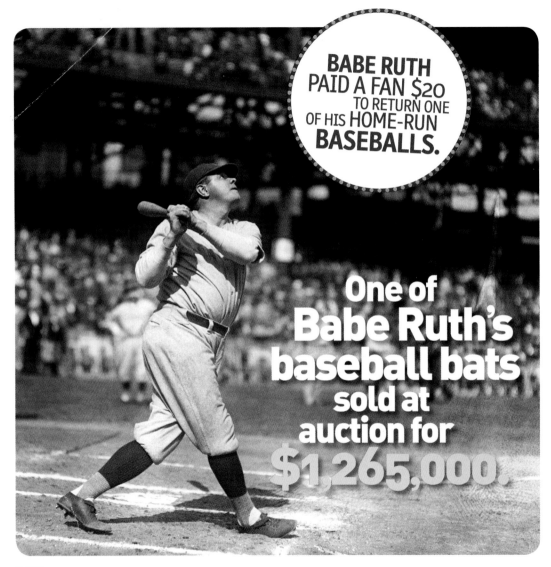

BABE RUTH PAID A FAN $20 TO RETURN ONE OF HIS HOME-RUN BASEBALLS.

One of **Babe Ruth's** baseball bats sold at auction for **$1,265,000.**

THE MOST HULA HOOPS SPUN AT ONE TIME: 200

A ROCK GROUP ONCE BANNED **BROWN M&M's** FROM BACKSTAGE AT THEIR CONCERTS.

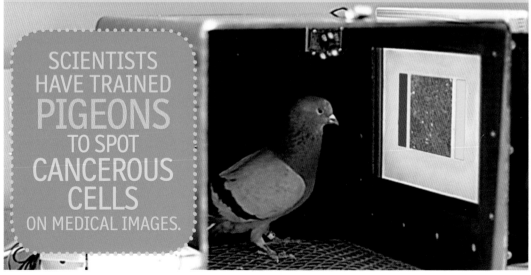

SCIENTISTS HAVE TRAINED **PIGEONS** TO SPOT **CANCEROUS CELLS** ON MEDICAL IMAGES.

TAYLOR
SWIFT
"DARE TO BE DIFFERENT"

2015

A **FARM** IN
MARYLAND, U.S.A.,
CREATED A
CORN MAZE
IN THE SHAPE OF
SINGER TAYLOR
SWIFT'S FACE.

SUMMERS FARM

AN ARTIST USED 17,625 GUMBALLS TO RE-CREATE TAYLOR SWIFT'S FACE.

Mantis shrimp
send each other **secret** messages using **light** signals.

A lunch menu
from the
R.M.S. Titanic
sold for
$88,000
in an
online auction.

In Massachusetts, U.S.A.,
it is illegal to dance to
"The Star-Spangled
Banner."

WORMS
THE SIZE OF
SNAKES
WERE FOUND
ON A REMOTE
SCOTTISH
ISLAND.

MOST OF EARTH'S SPECIES ARE STILL UNDISCOVERED.

More than **100 baseballs** are used in one **Major League Baseball game.**

IT CAN TAKE UP TO 21 DAYS TO MAKE A SINGLE JELLY BEAN.

YOU CAN BUY EARMUFFS MADE FROM ROADKILL.

Scientists found nearly 100 species of bacteria 30,000 feet (9,144 m) in the air.

A STUDY FOUND THAT **CHILDREN WHO GROW UP AROUND DOGS** HAVE A LOWER **RISK OF ASTHMA** THAN KIDS WHO AREN'T EXPOSED TO DOGS.

THE **TRASH** WE DUMP INTO THE OCEAN ANNUALLY WEIGHS **THREE TIMES MORE** THAN ALL THE FISH WE CATCH EACH YEAR.

MICROBES IN YOUR GUT TELL YOUR BRAIN WHEN YOU'RE FULL.

DURING THE U.S. CIVIL WAR, LOLLIPOPS WERE SOMETIMES MADE OF HARD CANDY STUCK TO THE END OF A PENCIL.

Scientists think that **Jupiter bumped a planet out of our solar system four billion years ago.**

A SCIENTIST USED MICROBES IN PETRI DISHES TO RE-CREATE

A FAMOUS VINCENT VAN GOGH PAINTING.

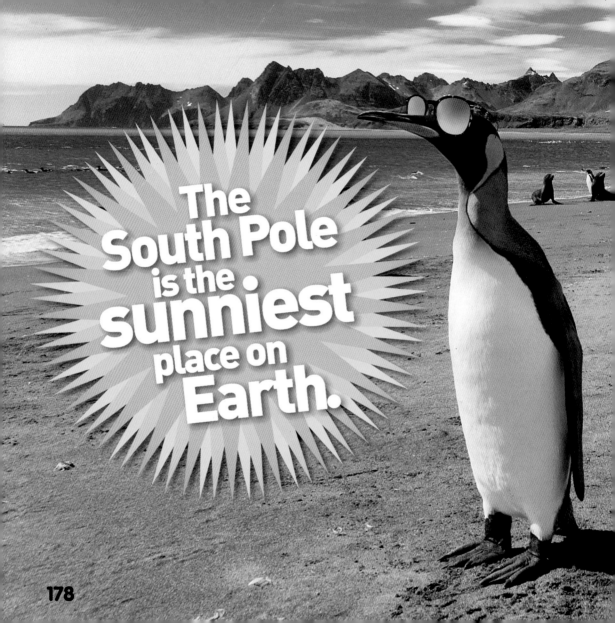

The
South Pole
is the
sunniest
place on
Earth.

Scientists nicknamed a new species of **peacock spider** **Sparklemuffin.**

The Caspian Sea is actually a lake.

Spider-Man would need sticky pads covering **40 percent** of his body to be able to scale walls, **one study found.**

RESIDENTS OF BARNAUL, SIBERIA, **CAMPAIGNED TO** ELECT A **CAT** AS THEIR MAYOR.

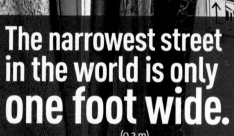

The narrowest street in the world is only **one foot wide.**
(0.3 m)

A KID HAD A LEGO PIECE STUCK UP HIS NOSE FOR THREE YEARS.

AN ASTEROID NAMED SPOOKY FLEW PAST EARTH ON HALLOWEEN.

THE EARLIEST
VERSION OF THE
PENNY SAID
" **MIND YOUR
BUSINESS**,"
NOT " *IN GOD
WE TRUST.* "

IT COSTS 1.7 CENTS
TO MAKE A PENNY.

THE FIRST COMPUTER PROGRAM WAS WRITTEN IN 1842.

IN CALIFORNIA, U.S.A., THERE IS A MUSEUM DEDICATED ENTIRELY TO **BANANAS.**

A MUSEUM IN OREGON, U.S.A., HAS A COLLECTION OF **300 VACUUMS.**

FACTFINDER

Boldface indicates illustrations.

FACTFINDER

asthma 172
cancer detection 163, **163**
from cockroaches 45, **45**
fake vomit 9
fidgeting 78
heart surgery, by robots 26, **26**
human spit as 9
from rain forest plants 67, **67**
ribs from 3-D printer 102
from sewer water mold 195, **195**
Mercury (planet) 9
Metal, world's lightest 153, **153**
Metric system 128
Mexico 142–143, **142–143**
Micro-robots 6
Microbes 175, **175**, 177, **177**
Microlattice (metal) 153, **153**
Milk, camel 93, **93**
Minnesota, U.S.A. 12, **12**
M&M's 163, **163**
Mold 195, **195**
"Mona Lisa" 139, **139**
Money 66, **66**, 187, **187**
Monopoly (board game) 43, **43**
Moon 158, 193, **193**
Moonbows 40–41, **40–41**
Mosquitoes 37, **37**, 73, **73**
Muscles 86, **86**, 121
Museums 198–199, **198–199**
Mushrooms 28, **28–29**, 121, **121**
Music 74, 84, 102
Musical canine freestyle 72, **72**

N

Names 63
National Moldy Cheese Day 127, **127**

Native Americans 158
Neanderthals 30
New England clam chowder 134, **134**
New Mexico State University 33
New Zealand 63, 75, **75**, 122
North Pole 21
North Pole, Alaska, U.S.A. 90
Noses 183, **183**, **196–197**, 197
Nuclear power plants 24

O

Obama, Barack 128
Oceans 100–101, **100–101**, 174
Octopuses 148–149, **148–149**
Oklahoma, U.S.A. 98, **98**
Olympic Games 62, **62**, 67
Onions, on fire 157, **157**
Ontario, Canada 130, **130–131**
Orchids 73, **73**
Oregon, U.S.A. 199, **199**
Oxygen 122

P

Paddling, in pumpkin 7, **7**
Painting 67
Pancakes 20, **20**, 57, **57**
Paper, oldest 135, **135**
Parachuting, by beavers 19, **19**
Peach pits, fossilized 151
Peacock spiders 180, **180**
Pee and peeing 15, 30, 86
Peekaboo 111
Pencils, as lollipop sticks 175, **175**
Penguins **178–179**
Pennies 187, **187**

Penny farthing (bicycle) 58, **58–59**
Pharaohs, female 45, **45**
Phelps, Michael 62, **62**
Philtrum 154–155, **154–155**
Phloem 85, **85**
Pigeons 163, **163**
Pigs 8, **8**, 42, **42**
Pilots 132
Pink lemonade 147, **147**
Pips 102, **102**
Pizza 79, **79**, 138, **138**
Plano, Texas, U.S.A 158, **158**
Plants
boats made from 13, **13**
carnivorous 39
on diamond deposits 36, **36**
fertilized by urine 30
fevers in 90
learning 75, **75**
medicine from 67, **67**
number of trees **34–35**, 35
pollination 64–65
sense of hearing 33, **33**
talking to one another 15
as toothbrush 30
Plastic shade balls 160, **160–161**
Pluto (dwarf planet) 110
Polar bears **92**
Polar regions 21
Pollination 64–65
Poodles 120, **120**
Poop 153, 198, **198**
Postage stamps 138, **138**
Potato, duck-shaped 144, **144**
Prairie dogs **88–89**, 89
Presidents of the United States

FACTFINDER

Since 1888, the National Geographic Society has funded more than 12,000 research, exploration, and preservation projects around the world. The Society receives funds from National Geographic Partners LLC, funded in part by your purchase. A portion of the proceeds from this book supports this vital work.

For more information, visit www.natgeo.com/info, call 1-800-647-5463, or write to the following address:
National Geographic Partners
1145 17th Street N.W.
Washington, D.C. 20036-4688 U.S.A.

Visit us online at nationalgeographic.com/books

For librarians and teachers:
ngchildrensbooks.org

More for kids from National Geographic:
kids.nationalgeographic.com

For information about special discounts for bulk purchases, please contact National Geographic Books Special Sales:
ngspecsales@ngs.org

For rights or permissions inquiries, please contact National Geographic Books Subsidiary Rights: ngbookrights@ngs.org

Designed by Rachael Hamm Plett, Moduza Design
Art direction by Jülide Obuz Dengel

Paperback ISBN: 978-1-4263-2559-5
Reinforced library binding ISBN:
978-1-4263-2560-1

Printed in China
16/PPS/1

The publisher would like to thank: Jen Agresta, for expertly tackling the project management and editing of this bizarre book; Hillary Leo of Royal Scruff, for her fantastic, yet still weird, photo editing skills; and Avery Hurt and Jeannette Swain, for diving headfirst into the world of wacky by researching and writing these truly strange facts.

PHOTO CREDITS

All artwork by MODUZA DESIGN unless otherwise noted below:

Cover and spine, Eric Isselée/Shutterstock; 2, Eric Isselée/Shutterstock; 4-5, Pal Teravagimov/Shutterstock; 7, Marc Vasconcellos/The Enterprise; 8, yevgeniy/Shutterstock; 10-11, EPA/DPA/Corbis; 12, Danita Delimont/Alamy; 13, All Canada Photos/Alamy; 16-17, Fairfax Media/Getty Images; 19 (background), Universal Images/Getty Images; 19 (UP), Ensuper/Shutterstock; 19 (LO LE), Christian Musat/Shutterstock; 19 (LO RT), Jnjhuz/Dreamstime; 19 (CTR), Aleksei Lazukov/Shutterstock; 21, djgis/Shutterstock; 22-23, Dave Watts/NPL/Minden Pictures; 24, Ethan Daniels/Shutterstock; 27, NASA; 28-29 (background), FotograFFF/Shutterstock; 29, Isselée/Dreamstime.com; 30, Newcastle University, UK; 32, Jim Brandenburg/Minden Pictures; 34-35, irin-k/Shutterstock; 37, Yves Adams/Getty Images; 38, DM7/Shutterstock; 39 (UP), Sagamore Hill National Historic Site; 39 (LO), Sari ONeal/Shutterstock; 40-41, Toshi Sasaki/Getty Images; 42, iStockphoto/Getty Images; 45, skydie/Shutterstock; 46 (UP LE), Flickr RM/Getty Images; 46 (LO LE), r.nagy/Shutterstock; 46-47 (background), Donovan van Staden/Shutterstock; 50, NASA; 52, Sonsedska Yuliia/Shutterstock; 52-53 (background), iStockphoto/Getty Images; 54, Gorawut Thuanmuang/Shutterstock; 55, AlexussK/Shutterstock; 57, Michael Bahlo/Newscom; 58-59, Matej Divizna/Getty Images; 60 (LE), Zigzag Mountain Art/Shutterstock; 60 (RT), courtesy Todd Anderson/Autobahn Tuning; 62, Everett Collection/Shutterstock; 64-65, iStockphoto/Getty Images; 66, NASA; 68, Missouri History Museum, St. Louis; 68 (LO LE and RT), The Sun photo/Shutterstock; 70 (LO), David Lentz/Getty Images; 70-71, siambizkit/Shutterstock; 72, Friso Gentsch/Newscom; 73, Nathalie Speliers/Shutterstock; 74, National Geographic Creative/Getty Images; 75, courtesy Golf Cross France; 76-77, Retna/Photoshot/Newscom; 78, Djama86/Dreamstime; 79, Europics/Instagram/newspix.com; 80, MarcelClemens/Shutterstock; 82-83, Cyril Ruoso/Minden Pictures; 85, iStockphoto/Getty Images; 86, iStockphoto/Getty Images; 88-89, iStockphoto/Getty Images; 91, Ron Gravelle; 92 (CTR), iStockphoto/Getty Images; 92 (UP), PeskyMonkey/Getty Images; 93, courtesy of the Zoological Society of London; 94-95, Magda Sayeg; 96, Wendy White/Alamy; 98, SOMMAI/Shutterstock; 99, solarseven/Shutterstock; 100-

101, Sarawut Kundej/Shutterstock; 102, Fiore/Shutterstock; 103, NASA; 104, Volt Collection/Shutterstock; 106, Library of Congress Prints and Photographs Division; 107 (LE), Dan Thornberg/Shutterstock; 107 (RT), photoDISC; 109, SWNS Group/Newscom; 110, Bunpot/Shutterstock; 112-113, D. Trozzo/Alamy; 117 (LO), John Karmali/FLPA/Minden Pictures; 117 (UP), Dja65/Dreamstime.com; 118-119, Huguette Roe/Shutterstock; 120, Kirkgeisler/Dreamstime.com; 125, courtesy Bubble Show by Mat j Kodes; 126, Rita Kochmarjova/Shutterstock; 127, ValentynVolkov/Getty Images; 128, Chuck Kennedy/Rapport Press/Newscom; 129, Wrangel/Dreamstime; 130-131, Newscom; 133, Franco Tempesta; 134, iStockphoto/Getty Images; 135, courtesy Pierre Tallet, Sorbonne; 136-137, Food Centrale Hamburg GmbH/Alamy; 139, Maurice Bennett, Supplied by PacificCoastNews/Newscom; 142-143, Witold Skrypczak/Getty Images; 144, James Curley/REX/Newscom; 145, courtesy Ronald Reagan Library; 146, Olga Selyutina/Shutterstock; 147, courtesy Dr. David Gruber, National Geographic Emerging Explorer; 148-149, iStockphoto/Getty Images; 150, sergioboccardo/Shutterstock; 153, Photo by Dan Little HRL Laboratories, LLC; 154-155, Blend Images/Shutterstock; 156, Courtesy Kathy Townsend, University of Queensland; 159, Everett Collection; 160-161, AP Photo/Damian Dovargane; 161, AP Photo/Damian Dovarganes; 162, Bettmann/Corbis; 163, courtesy Edward A. Wasserman, University of Iowa; 164, courtesy Jeff Greenwood, Summers Farm; 165, Rob Surette, Hero Art; 166, Whitcomberd/Dreamstime; 168, NHPA/Photoshot/Newscom; 170, Dan Thornberg/Shutterstock; 172-173, Marina Jay/Shutterstock; 175, BSIP/UIG/Getty Images; 176, David Aguilar; 177, courtesy Melanie Sullivan; 178-179, Gen Productions/Shutterstock; 178-179 (CTR), visivastudio/Shutterstock; 179 (LO), Keith Homan/Shutterstock; 180, Jurgen Otto; 181, Anton Balazh/Shutterstock; 183 (LE), NRT/Shutterstock; 183 (RT), EPA/Newscom; 184-185, Melvinlee/Dreamstime.com; 187, welzevoul/Shutterstock; 189, Jeffrey Mayer/Wireimag/Getty Images; 190-191, Mary Evans Picture Library/Alamy; 194, Luke Sharrett/Bloomber/Getty Images; 195 (UP), Nataliia K/Shutterstock; 195 (LO), Alptraum/Dreamstime; 196-197, 1999 EyeWire, Inc.

Totally WEIRD
(but maybe NOT true!)

Can you tell the truth from a tall tale? Spot a fib or a phony in five seconds flat? Put your amateur detective skills to the test in this fun book. Give it a try . . . spot the lie!

NATIONAL GEOGRAPHIC KiDS
REAL OR FAKE?
FAR-OUT FIBS, FISHY FACTS, AND PHONY PHOTOS TO TEST FOR THE TRUTH

EMILY KRIEGER
ILLUSTRATIONS BY TOM NICK COCOTOS

IDENTIFY THE LIE!

For each question group below, two statements are TRUE, and one is FALSE. Can you put your finger on the fib?

1
A. Ancient Romans used urine as mouthwash.

B. Tiger cubs are born furless and without any stripes.

C. Tiny critters called book scorpions live in the pages of old books.

2
A. You can mail a coconut without packaging it.

B. A flock of ravens is called an unkindness.

C. A pizza topped with flamingo and dormouse was found buried with Julius Caesar.

34